Saving Super Mom

Saving Super Mom

KRISTI WALTERS

WESTBOW
PRESS
A DIVISION OF THOMAS NELSON

WestBow Press books may be ordered through booksellers or by contacting:

WestBow Press
A Division of Thomas Nelson
1663 Liberty Drive
Bloomington, IN 47403
www.westbowpress.com
1-(866) 928-1240

Because of the dynamic nature of the Internet, any web addresses or links contained in this book may have changed since publication and may no longer be valid. The views expressed in this work are solely those of the author and do not necessarily reflect the views of the publisher, and the publisher hereby disclaims any responsibility for them.

Images property of Kristi Walters. Cover design by Holly Hollon Design & Calligraphy
Author photo by Heather Cummans Photography
Any people depicted in stock imagery provided by Thinkstock are models,
and such images are being used for illustrative purposes only.

ISBN: 978-1-4497-2721-5 (e)
ISBN: 978-1-4497-2720-8 (sc)

Library of Congress Control Number: 2011917009

Printed in the United States of America

WestBow Press rev. date: 12/14/2011

Contents

In support of the Birmingham Dream Center

The Birmingham Dream Center is located in the heart of the historic Woodlawn Community in downtown Birmingham. Our mission is to share the love of Christ with individuals, serve our community and advance God's Kingdom.

From tutoring students in local schools, to adopting a street in our community, there are many varied opportunities to serve with us. Please visit www.birminghamdreamcenter.com for more information on how to connect.

Suggested Study Outline

Week One
  Read Chapters 1 & 2
  Homework Assignment 1; turn in assignment to leader
  Group discussion of completed reading and assignment
Week Two
  Read Lesson 1 and answer questions
  Complete Homework Assignment 2
  Group discussion of completed Week Two reading and homework
Week Three
  Read Lesson 2
  Complete Homework Assignment 3
  Choose a verse to claim and pray for your child for the next year
  Group discussion of completed Week Three reading and homework
Week Four
  Read Lesson 3 and answer questions
  Read Lesson 4 and answer questions
  Complete Homework Assignment 4; items 1 through 3
  Group discussion of completed Week Four reading and homework.
  Leader returns Homework Assignment 1 (Ideal Week from Tool
  Kit) to group members.
  Homework items 4 through 7 to be completed during group meeting
Week Five
  Read Lesson 5 and answer questions
  Complete Homework Assignment 5
  Group discussion
Week Six
  Read Lesson 6 and answer questions
  Complete Homework Assignment 6
  Group discussion
Week Seven
  Read Lesson 7 and answer questions
  Complete Homework Assignment 7
  Group discussion

Week Eight

> Read Lesson 8
>
> Review and refine Sections 3, 4 and 5 from Tool Kit
>
> Complete Homework Assignment 8
>
> Group discussion. Using all the information from Tool Kit and sharing ideas, discuss best ways to successfully complete Assignment 8

Future

> Form accountability group or partners to help one another stay on task, reach goals and live out vision statements
>
> Meet regularly to share super mom secrets and time saving ideas

Acknowledgements

I would like to extend a heartfelt thanks to the women's ministries team at Trinity on the Hill United Methodist Church in Augusta, Georgia. I am especially grateful to Kimberly, who first introduced me to the concept of time management as a bible study through the *Roles and Goals* curriculum, to Lisa, who held me accountable and to Kris for the education and inspiration.

I am now grateful to be a part of Church of the Highlands where vision, leadership and trail blazing are encouraged.

Most importantly, to my husband, David, and children, Alli, Grayson, Natalie and Haydin, who are my constant motivation, thank you.

Part 1:

Will the Real Super Mom Please Stand Up?

Chapter 1:
Life on Planet Krypton

It's 6:50 a.m., and my alarm clock is going nuts. Beep, beep, beep. But it's not just any beep. It's a high-pitched, long sort of beep, just like the beeping you hear when a Mack truck is warning you that it is backing up.

I'm so tired. I don't want to get up because I just got into a good sleep around 5:00 a.m. Last night I stayed up until after midnight returning e-mails and going through piles of mail while baking beautifully decorated, blue, butterfly-shaped butter cookies to celebrate the letter "B." You see, the next day was special snack day and it was my turn to provide the treat. Each week a different letter, color or theme was studied in my child's classroom. The teacher, Mrs. Barfield, was remarkable. All week long anything associated with the theme was turned into a learning opportunity. The highlight of the theme came on Friday when one child's mom brought special snack. Every Friday afternoon when the children were picked up from school, the parents got a detailed report of what the special snack was and whose mom brought it. Some of the snacks were fabulous and some were flops. Trust me, no one wanted to be one of the flops.

Why would I wait until the last minute to start such an important project? I didn't start until 9:00 p.m. because after I had helped with homework, prepared a well-balanced meal, cleaned the kitchen, bathed the children, and put them to bed, I ran out of daylight hours. My entire day had been spent running to and fro like a ping-pong ball in play at a world championship match. The paddles that bounce me back and forth are made up of grocery lists, Bible studies, committee meetings, play dates, school performances, sporting events, lunch dates, diaper changes, art projects, carpools, toys, spills, and a part-time job.

My plan was to get in bed at midnight so that I could sleep for nearly seven hours before I had to get up. I fall into bed completely exhausted, make a nice neck roll out of the bottom edge of my pillow, throw the comforter off the end of the bed, and cover up with only the sheet and blanket nicely tucked over my shoulders. Dreamland at last.

A mere sixty seconds into the sleep zone and my eyes pop open. My mind races. I am orchestrating the events of tomorrow with great timing and precision. I can do this master jigsaw puzzle because I am "Super Mom." Then the worry creeps in. Satan catches me awake and starts conjuring up doubt. "Okay, Satan, you don't scare me. You have no authority over me." But in his persistent way, he continues to taunt me.

"How am I going to pay all those bills sitting on the desk? What should I send for Show and Tell? Didn't my husband hear that noise outside?" My thoughts go on and on.

Finally, free of thought, I fall asleep. "Mom," calls a little voice from upstairs. Then I hear coughing. "I need a drink of water." The last thing I remember are the glowing orange numbers on the clock that read 4:58 a.m.

Beep! Beep! Beep! I hit the snooze button. Just seven more minutes, *please*. Then, what seems like only a moment later, the beeping resumes. That Mack truck is backing right into the side of my mattress.

Exhausted, yet full of confidence, I get out of bed visualizing a big "S" on my chest and reach for my red superhero cape. Suddenly I realize that "Super Mom" has forgotten that one child has a field trip today, for which I have to make a lunch, and the required school-identifying T-shirt is in the dirty hamper. And we don't have enough milk for breakfast.

What a crazy way to live! But that's exactly what I did. I was running frantically on a treadmill of over-commitment and super-achievement—rarely breaking a sweat. The sleepless nights, frenzied morning routine, and exhausting scramble to pull every small detail together were well concealed from the outside world. I just showed up with a smile and played the part of Polly Perfect. I had to afford my children every conceivable opportunity while maintaining the facade of a perfect home life and a solid reputation as a good friend and faithful servant of Christ.

And the thing is, I was pretty good at it. So good that I could shift into autopilot and cruise through the day with what seemed to be storybook perfection. Why? Because I'm Super Mom, and everything here on planet Krypton plays out like a Norman Rockwell painting . . . or at least it appears that way.

I began to seriously question myself. In all of this success, what part of it was truly valuable? How much of this success was invested in the kingdom rather than the world? How long could I live in this concealed state of frailty?

The problem was that there was more of me doing the work than the Father. I had managed to smother—with obligations and expectations—the freedom given to me by the Holy Spirit. I was always tired and had little manageable margin to work with if one of my little duckies got out of its row. I was running on empty, too busy to ever stop and refuel.

What I needed to do was to get out of my own way. First, God would need to be in charge of my agenda. After all, He created the world in six days. I'm pretty sure that He could get my kindergartener to school on time.

Second, I needed to let God show me what my priorities should be. The end goal would be of His choosing, and I would manage my time according to His purpose. Then the pretty package on the outside would more accurately reflect the contents on the inside. My eyes would be open to the opportunities He placed before me. What could be better than to live within God's will for your life? I decided it was time to re-evaluate.

Not long after changing my perspective, I received a phone call from Liza Kittle, a women's ministry coordinator from my church in Augusta, Georgia. She called to ask if I would consider getting involved with helping the church leadership team plan a community-wide women's event. I was asked to take a couple of days to prayerfully consider her offer before I answered.

Truthfully, old habits die hard. I would have committed right away. Liza didn't need to ask me to wait a couple of days. Looking back, this was my first lesson in seeking God's will before making a personal commitment. The desire to better serve my church had already been stirring in me. But those two days gave me the opportunity to actively seek God's will for my service.

I served on this leadership committee for two years. I ended up being in charge of public relations for women's ministries, which had evolved into a group called, Women of the Vine. However, I did not want to do PR. Frankly, I was sick of it. I had spent my entire professional career doing PR and marketing, and I wanted to do something new. Foolishly, I thought that the success or, worse, failure of an event or campaign was directly related to the success or failure of my efforts. It was too much pressure. I was obviously having a hard time getting over the concept that I was the one who had to do all the work.

Reverend Kris Key, minister of discipleship at our church, led the leadership meetings. Kris was one of the most prayerful women I'd ever met. She prayed out everything. On Sunday mornings when she led the prayer for our congregation, you could see that the Holy Spirit consumed her. Her countenance was graceful, and she had an open and direct link to the Father. If the entire congregation had gotten up and walked out of the sanctuary during prayer, she would not have noticed. Her eyes were fixed on God and she was in communion with Him.

At our very first organizational meeting, we were presented with several roles that needed to be filled. Among them were intercession, resources, hospitality, PR, and more. We each had a three-by-five note card, and we were supposed to write down the area to which we were being called. I was all fired up to write down something like "decorating" or "lunch," but no. Kris would not let us write on the card. She made us wait. When we finally could write something, we had to write down a gift, a talent, or an experience. Then she made us meditate and listen for God's voice. And then we prayed. And then we meditated some more. Prayed more. Listened more.

Here's what was going on in my head: "I am not going to do PR. I always get stuck with PR. Someone else in this room is being called to do PR, and they just need to speak up. I throw a really good party. I need to do hospitality."

After all that praying and meditating, this is what God said: "Surely you don't think that I have given you this gift and allowed you the experience of your career that you might waste it? I groomed you in this way for my higher, heavenly purpose. Do you love me enough to obey?"

I wrote "PR" on my card and turned it in.

Two significant things happened during the two years that I served in women's ministries. First, Kris had the leadership team go through intense leadership training titled "Lead Like Jesus." This program had some prerequisites that required serious self-examination and the development of a personal mission statement or vision for your life.

Second, my dear friend, Kimberly Knox, shared with a small group of women some information from a seminar she had attended called "Roles & Goals: Using God's Time Wisely." Using a couple of tips and tools from this resource and the vision statement work from "Lead Like Jesus," I developed a daily plan for my life.

I was already a highly organized person with lofty goals. Now all the pieces of this puzzle suddenly clicked together in my mind. I took a big step back and looked at the details that made up my whole life. I questioned my priorities and let go of the things that were dragging me down—even the good stuff. I began to seek God's direction for every hour of my day, as I had been made to do on "note card day" at the first women's committee meeting. This exercise revolutionized my quiet time. I could see and hear God like never before. I started dropping things from my schedule left and right; things like multiple play groups, club memberships, various leadership positions and activities that overlapped one another. Ultimately, I found that I did much more in less time compared to the way I had been living. I was able to seek Him more and do only those things that He would have me do. I discovered what it meant to yield my time to God, and the result was a fruitful harvest that benefitted my family as much as it benefitted me.

My life was good . . . really good. My family was thriving, I had great friends, I had the support of my church, and I loved the children's school and teachers. I even had perfect attendance at Bible study and Wednesday night church. I was so inspired that I knew I had to share what I had learned with other people.

A year later, I joined forces with my friend Kimberly, and we shared the information with a new group of people. To my surprise, it was quite a challenge to communicate the same revelation that I had received to others. There were too many moving parts and not enough structure.

However, the blessing in the challenge was the word I received from God. "Kristi, I am going to use *you* to write this study, develop the tools, and share it with my people." I was in good with God now. This would be easy. After all, it wasn't my idea. It was His.

Chapter 2:
Life on Planet Earth

Ha, ha, ha! Cocky, huh? Well, don't worry. I was humbled. Almost immediately, everything in my life changed. My husband got a new job and we were moving to Birmingham, Alabama. *Alabama!?*

I'll never forget the drive from Augusta to Birmingham. I cried. Actually, I bawled like a baby for the entire five-hour drive. I was seven months pregnant with my fourth child as I followed my husband down I-20 with an SUV full of loose junk and boxes. Since it was clearly his fault that we were moving, I found it more than irritating that he insisted on calling me every three minutes to check to see if I was okay. I felt that in a moment I had lost my home, all my friends, part of my family, my community, and my church.

I did, however, still have our pet rabbit, Snowflake. She was making the trip in the back of my SUV. I think Snowflake was a hero that day. To protect her, I did my very best to drive cautiously through the tears.

When the moving truck arrived in Birmingham with our furniture and most of our belongings, everything wouldn't fit in the tiny house we had rented. The things that wouldn't fit we left in the driveway and had the Jimmy Hale Mission pick up. It was a low moment.

It was also the moment that preceded my new, modern-day, southern-belle neighbor strolling past our front lawn to check out the new people. In a slightly nasal, deep southern drawl, she shouted out a three-syllable "Hi!" It sounded something like "Hi-ah-uh!" She continued on, "I'm Lexi. You're gonna *love it* here!" I did not exactly share her sentiments.

I blamed my husband for the move, scarcely considering that it might have been a pivotal point in God's plan for me. I think that I knew deep inside that God was still teaching me that I had to let go of *everything* (even the furniture) in order for Him to be in charge of it all.

But, being too stubborn to see the opportunity He had given me with a fresh, clean slate, I went into a self-inflicted state of depression and was unable to rally before the birth of my daughter, Haydin. She was born shortly after the move, and things really got bad.

For the entire first year of her life, Haydin cried all day long. If you have ever had a sleepless night because of a sick or crying newborn, you understand what I mean when I say that for the next 365 days, God shook me down.

Aside from the obvious lack of sleep and the frazzled nerves, the things in my life that I thought I could count on as my constants began to unravel. First of all, my husband, whom I thought would be more available after nearly eleven years of school and medical training, was traveling three out of five days a week to remote area hospitals, in addition to being on call a lot. My oldest daughter, Alli, known for her pleasant demeanor and exceptional academic achievements, completely lost interest in school. Grayson, my only son, was on the receiving end of some neighborhood bullying, and my three-year-old, Natalie, was having trouble making friends at her new preschool. I even had to drop out of my Bible study because I couldn't retain childcare for Haydin, (you know, the new baby who cried *all the time*).

Super Mom's reign was over. I found myself on the opposing side of my husband, teachers, neighbors, and other parents. There was seldom a family dinner, no friends to hang out with, no church home, and certainly not something as extravagant as that strange and unfamiliar thing called "date night." I rarely left the house and was just plain old S-A-D, sad. Sad, sad, sad, sad, and sad. If I had been given a chance to buy myself a break I could not have done it. Why? Because on top of everything else, we were flat broke. We had to start this new life from rock bottom, and we were looking straight uphill. I was no longer on Krypton, but had been hurled to planet Earth.

On one particular day I received a telephone call, and I saw my old neighbor's phone number on caller ID. Could this be a ray of sunshine in my current dark world? She had called to see how we were doing and give me updates on life in Augusta. During our conversation, she mentioned how beautifully the roses were doing in my old backyard. I had planted them near the picket fence that separated her yard from mine. For those whom have ever nurtured a rose garden, you understand the blood, sweat, and tears that go into it. Those were *my* roses. "Tons of gorgeous blooms," she continued. I hung up the phone and burst into tears.

Did I mention that I had been humbled? Downright, slap-in-the-face humbled. When you are absolutely at the bottom, where else do you go? I began with, "Jesus. I know you are there. I have no idea what to say. Help. Amen."

Every day I prayed a little more. I loosened my grasp on all the "stuff" I was hanging on to so tightly. I prayed and prayed until finally I realized that I had regained everything that I had lost.

What I regained wasn't my home; it wasn't my social life or my position in the church and community. I still didn't have my children in well-matched, cleaned, and pressed outfits, surrounding the prepared feast at the dinner table as my husband arrived joyfully home from work. What I had regained was full and open communication with God. The most important relationship in my life had been restored. That was everything, because everything else hinged on it.

Then, one day, the baby just stopped crying. It was like the sky parted and I could see light again. Can't you just hear the chorus to "Hallelujah"? The vision for writing this book was reborn. I realized I had been through a refinement process in order to be able to complete the task empty of me, but full of God. God truly does work all things together for good. I have to give credit first to Him and then to all of the previously mentioned people and events (both good and catastrophic) for finally bringing this book and study guide together. I am thankful to be on the path of my God-inspired vision.

The following chapters are a collection of lessons I've learned while being at the top of the Super Mom game and while sitting at the bottom of the batting order on the Super Mom sideline. Your perspective of time management, priorities, and goals will be challenged. You will evaluate all the roles God has given you in all aspects of your life. And, if you open up, let go, and allow God to shake you down a little at a time, you will live your calling and define your time on earth according to His purpose. You will save Super Mom.

Homework Assignment 1:

1. Go to Part 3 of this book. This is your Tool Kit.
2. Using Section 1 of your Tool Kit, entitled "Weekly Agendas," fill in the blanks of the "Ideal Week" agenda with what you perceive to be a perfect week. Be sure to use up the whole twenty-four hours for all seven days.
3. Once complete, do not look at the "Ideal Week" agenda again until directed to do so.
4. To maximize the effectiveness of this exercise, it is best to completely fill out this agenda *right now.*

Part 2:

The Lessons

Lesson 1:
Time Management 101

"I'm late! I'm late! For a very important date! No time to say 'hello,' good-bye! I'm late! I'm late! I'm late!"[1] I hear the White Rabbit's words a lot. I hear them because he actually lives in the dashboard of my car. He stays hidden behind the digital clock on my car stereo. The funny thing is that the White Rabbit does not know that the clock in my car is exactly eight minutes ahead of real time. Therefore, I can drop a kid off at her or his destination and still have approximately six minutes to spare.

Those six minutes are invaluable. I need the margin, for one child in particular, to get almost to where they need to be, realize what they forgot, run back to the car in sheer panic mode, frantically collect the missing item, regroup, and finally join the activity on time. You can try and try to teach the lesson, and sometimes it's learned, but it's always good to keep that little white rabbit scurrying.

On a serious note, though, those six minutes really are exceedingly valuable. I read a quotation once that perfectly sums up time: "Time is at once the most valuable and the most perishable of all our possessions."[2] Time given in this life is precious because it is given in a finite amount. Once used, time can never be restored or regained. Neither race nor status, knowledge nor power has any effect on this fact. A unit of time is measured the same way for everyone. What isn't the same for everyone is the activity that occurs during that unit of time.

Merriam-Webster defines time as "a measurable period during which an action, process or condition exists or continues; a non-spatial continuum that is measured in terms of events which succeed one

---

[1]   http//Disney.wikia.com/wiki/I'm Late
[2]   John Randolph, U.S. Senator 1825-1827

15

another from past through present to future." It is also defined as a person's experience during a specified period or a particular occasion.[3]

It sounds boring and overly scientific, but this definition is really quite profound. It takes into account a set of circumstances to be managed and links the measurement of time to events as they move one to another. More significantly, it relates a person's perspective of existence to a specified period of time. It gives time quality and substance.

In Webster's definition of time, however, there is a particularly crucial piece of information that is missing. Webster does not mention that all time has been preordained by its Creator. Every second makes up the hours of a day planned by God before time, as we know it, existed. Collectively, those days make up a *life* that has been ordered by its Creator. Our life, our time, has meaning. It is more than a random collection of incidents that occur between birth and death. Therefore, we must live with purpose and intention.

> Our life, our time, has meaning. It is more than a random collection of incidents between birth and death. Therefore, **we must live with purpose and intention.**

In Acts 17:26-28 NIV, Paul clearly states, "From one man he made every nation of men, that they should inhabit the whole earth; and he determined the times set for them and the exact places where they should live. God did this so that men would seek him and perhaps reach out for him and find him, though he is not far from each one of us. 'For in him we live and move and have our being.'"

According to the Scripture, is there any person, any place, to whom this does not apply? Well, I exist, so it certainly applies to me.

On January 19, 1996, I married the tall, dark, and totally hot frat boy I met in college, David Walters. I actually didn't think that I would ever get married, and even if I did, it would be somewhere between 2002 and 2005. But God knew the exact time and date of the event. He even knew that it would be one of the coldest days on record in Dallas, Texas, in a decade of winters.

To me, that day was the first day of our journey together on the "Five-Year Plan." The Five-Year Plan was my basic observation of

---

[3] By permission. From *Merriam-Webster's Collegiate® Dictionary 11th Edition©* *2011* by Merriam-Webster Incorporated (www.merriam-webster.com)

how happy, successful couples in our peer group approached marriage. Specifically, the five-year period in reference is the time between marriage and your first child. That's also when you and all your friends were what we called "dinks" back then (double income, no kids). As a couple, you both spend all your time working outrageous, pay-your-dues type hours in order to amass the largest nest egg possible. Approximately two years later, you both get promotions, and by year three, you purchase your first home. The fourth year is spent furnishing your new home, and approaching year five, you start making plans to turn the home office into a nursery. Three months into year five, you are pregnant with your first child, and by the day of the big arrival, the Five-Year Plan is complete. Then it's off to trade in your BMW roadster for a minivan.

As it turned out, the joke was on me. This plan did not even resemble God's plan. Immediately after the wedding, I moved from Dallas to Austin, where we got our first apartment together. I had resigned from my job in Dallas and started my own business out of my home in Austin. It wasn't too fancy or all that impressive; I had merely relocated and contracted myself back to the company where I had been employed two weeks before the wedding. This was easy to do, but it did not pay well because I did not have that much work in my new role. The double income thing wasn't working out like I had imagined.

By springtime, things had changed significantly. David quit his job and enrolled at the University of Texas as a pre-med student. I worked through the summer while he attended classes. When the fall semester approached, however, we were told that David actually had not enrolled in time to continue with his studies in Austin during the fall semester. The enrollment period for the fall had been back around the beginning of the year. He could instead transfer to the Dallas campus, but classes started in a week.

At this point, we had totally abandoned the Five-Year Plan and had no choice but to boldly step out in faith wherever God told us to go. It seemed clear that He was telling us to go back to Dallas. So, in a day, we broke our apartment lease, rented a U-haul truck, loaded everything we owned and headed north on I-35.

We did not really have a place to go. We were just driving. We pulled up in front of the house where David grew up. His mother lived there alone, and the house was on the market. We simply humbled ourselves and asked for a place to stay.

The next day, we went to the campus to get David enrolled in classes. He already had a business degree from Baylor University, so he only needed the required science classes to make an application to medical school. He was a late enrollee, and the classes available were extremely limited. We both took it as a sign of confirmation from the Lord that the exact classes he needed were the only ones with openings still available, and not one of them overlapped in day or time.

We moved some of our belongings into David's childhood home and the rest into a storage facility. The house had been put on the market only a couple of weeks prior to our arrival. At that time, in this particular area of Dallas, real estate wasn't moving. Houses were sitting on the market for a year or more. We thought that this would buy us some time.

Wrong! The house sold and closed right away. We were homeless and jobless for a small stint, but we kept doing what God was telling us to do and He provided. Six months later, and ten years before David finished his residency, God revealed phase two of His plan. Surprise! I was going to have a baby . . . in about six months. I had been pregnant for approximately eleven weeks at that point. Don't ask how a woman can get through a whole trimester and not know she is pregnant. It can happen. It happened to me.

My point is this—my plan looked nothing like God's plan. I didn't know I would start a business, become a wife and a mother, or drive across Texas with my life in the back of a U-Haul. But *He* did. It was scripted out before I was a twinkle in my mother's eye. Paul said it right there in Acts 17. The Lord created me, my time and my place. "For in Him we live and move and have our being."

The most perfect example of purposefully living a life ordained by God is the life of Jesus himself. Jesus certainly understood that His life, His time, was not His own, but the Father's.

Examine Jesus' perspective of His time on earth by completing the following verses:

John 4:34 "My food," said Jesus,

John 5:30 By myself I can do nothing; I judge only as I hear, and my judgment is just, for

---

John 6:38 I have come down from heaven,

Through prayerful obedience, the indwelling Holy Spirit enables us to follow Jesus' example. If we abide in Him and seek His will in all things, our thoughts and desires begin to evolve. Our free will is brought into alignment with the persuasion of the Holy Spirit. Only then can we organize our time to live according to His calling in our lives.

Each of our actions is a step that ultimately leads to the plan God has for our lives. Everything we do, think, or say is bathed in His grace, and we put into place the building blocks that lead to His higher purpose—the stuff that gives our lives meaning.

> The first step in achieving alignment of our own will with that of the Holy Spirit is to come to a heart-surrendering agreement with the Lord that it is not our time, but God's. Our eyes are then opened to the truth that **His purpose is our purpose.**

Without this crucial alignment, we spin aimlessly through our daily agenda, marking off items on our "to-do" list. This process can go into autopilot and the days become weeks, the weeks become months, and in many cases the months become years. Though we may complete many fine projects and achieve great success, in due time the realization hits that we have built a grand-prize-winning castle made of sand. And eventually, the rain will come.

If you read this book and walk away with only one pearl of wisdom on time management, the most important thing would be the next paragraph:

The first step in achieving alignment of our own will with that of the Holy Spirit is to come to a heart-surrendering agreement with the Lord that it is not our time, but God's. Our eyes are then opened to the truth that His purpose is our purpose.

That is Time Management 101. It is the foundation of every goal we have, every task we schedule, and the very text on the road map of our lives.

Homework Assignment 2:

1. Using Section 1 of your Tool Kit, fill in the blanks of the "Week One" agenda *as each event occurs.* This will be a record of how you actually spend your time.
2. Keep this record with you this week and be sure to use up the whole twenty-four hours for each day. Do not look back at your "Ideal Week" for reference.
3. Do this exercise to the best of your ability for seven consecutive days.
4. Once complete, you should be ready to begin Lesson 2.

Lesson 2:
Quiet Time 101

Discovering the truth about time and its Author starts with the most basic essential of Christianity—a relationship with Christ. Seek Him. Worship Him. Speak to Him. Listen to Him. Love Him. *Make time for Him!* The practice of yielding our time back to the Creator, who predestined us to live for Him, is fundamental to managing and defining our time. With absolute resolve, we must commit ourselves to having a daily quiet time.

Billy Graham says the following about having a quiet time:

> The most important thing in our Christian lives is a daily walk with Christ, and that begins with your quiet time. Without a daily time of personal fellowship with Christ, it is likely that you will become a spiritual casualty in the next 10 years. Start the day with Christ. When you wake up, let your first thoughts be of Christ.[4]

A "spiritual casualty" . . . those are pretty strong words from a man whose opinion I sincerely respect. Strong words indeed, but I think he is exactly right. The neglect starts little by little and continues to expand. We oversleep one day and miss our quiet time. Then it's another day. We convince ourselves that we will push it to the afternoon, but something comes up that needs our immediate attention. Justifying the situation, we tell ourselves that it can be done at night once everyone is in bed. Oh, never mind. The baby is up all night crying and the opportunity has become lost. The next thing you know, there has been no personal quiet time with God in over a month.

---

[4]   Billy Graham, "Completing the Task God Gives Us" Decision Magazine, www.billygraham.org (October 1, 2008)

For me personally, God never lets it go too far without a huge wake-up call. He will always allow something to sneak up and catch my attention. Sometimes it is an enormous blessing that I clearly do not deserve that humbles me. Other times it is a great tragedy that leaves me with no hope but in Him. Most often, however, I am slowly awakened by the fact that I can't do anything on my own. I have pushed, pulled, strategized, manipulated, and worked until I have nothing left. After exhausting all possibilities, I finally turn to God in prayer.

When Grayson was very young, he had a difficult time controlling his emotions and behavior. Like most young mothers, I often found myself at my wit's end trying to train this child to behave. I was following all the rules, reading all the books, and implementing discipline. But boy, oh boy, sometimes we just had one of those days! None of the "expert" advice was working. I reviewed everything I knew about the mechanics of parenting. This wasn't my first child and I was not doing anything differently. I was at a total loss and found myself pleading with God over and over to make it stop.

Then I simply started praying 1 Thessalonians 5:6 in this way: "Lord, let Grayson be alert and self-controlled." Each time I prayed this verse, it was a sincere, heartfelt petition to God. I tracked these prayers and the surrounding circumstances in my prayer journal. Eventually I could see documented growth in this area. Grayson's actions and demeanor were positively affected. I was more able to enjoy the enormous blessing that God had given me with precious boy.

The process revolutionized my quiet time. Now each of my four children has their own verse that I pray for them. Initially, it cost me a little time selecting the verses, but once chosen, only a few seconds were required to use it. Moreover, these verses gave me an avenue by which I developed a consistent quiet time, and my personal relationship with Christ grew.

I also discovered a life lesson about the depth of using Scripture to pray. The verses have power because God's word is true, alive, and active. You can claim it for your children and pray it right into their lives. You can teach it to them and they can claim it for themselves.

When I can't form my own words to pray, Scripture enables me to speak about matters such as humility, wisdom, truthfulness, long-suffering, compassion, and strength. It makes my prayers for my children equivalent to God's desires for them. It plants God's word into my heart. That is the kind of thing God can do with the time we give Him.

> When I can't form my own words to pray, Scripture enables me to speak about matters such as humility, wisdom, truthfulness, long-suffering, compassion and strength. **It makes my prayers for my children equivalent to God's desires for them.**

If you are not currently practicing a regular quiet time, or if your time with God is not the quality experience it should be, start right now. As you work through the time management exercises in this study, you may discover some obstacles that have kept you from seeking God on a daily basis. Be willing to identify and remove them. There is no greater priority. Whatever your situation, making this time a priority is where a real relationship begins.

Let's go back to that most perfect example, Jesus. Write out the following verses:

Mark 1:35

_____

_____

Luke 5:16

_____

_____

Matthew 26:36

_____

_____

These verses, along with many other biblical examples, demonstrate three core elements that Jesus employed in his quiet time.

1. Jesus prayed early.
2. Jesus prayed often.
3. Jesus prayed alone.

When you first wake up in the morning, there is a whole lot of living in the world to be done over the next several hours. Therefore, it is optimal to have your quiet time early. This is what I recommend and what I try to do. But I am a flawed human living in the real world with everyone else, and sometimes I miss the mark.

The important thing to understand here is that "early" doesn't only mean at the crack of dawn or before the rest of the house is awake. It also means "before." Before making an important decision. Before imposing a discipline on your child. Before making a major purchase. Before Jesus set out to do anything, He consulted with the Father in prayer. Jesus was in constant communication with Him and acted in obedience to His Father's will.

There are many examples of Jesus praying to God with, for, and on behalf of the people, but He always made time to have one-on-one fellowship with Him. He directed His disciples away from Himself and went to places where He would be all alone and free of distraction. It was in the garden at Gethsemane that Jesus was alone with God and received the word that the time had come for Him to go to the cross to save the world.

What a message! Praise God for Jesus' faithfulness in constantly seeking Him. Because of Jesus, we can have that same intimate communication with the God of the Universe. His relationship was personal and ours is too. When we seek God daily, we get a game plan from the original Author of the playbook. That puts us in a winning position. Remember, we are living on His timeline, and He knows the right path for our feet.

King David, not knowing all that his future would hold, sought God's direction from moment to moment. In his days before becoming king, David, like us, lived in the real world. In Psalms, we find David being pursued by Saul, in fear of losing his life, battling hopelessness and depression, yet remaining in constant prayer and worship. Psalm 143:8-10 NIV is an awesome demonstration of David living out the same basic principles that Jesus did in seeking direction from the Father during his quiet time.

> Let the morning bring me word of your unfailing love,
> for I have put my trust in you.
> Show me the way I should go,
> for to you I lift up my soul.
> Rescue me from my enemies, O Lord,
> for I hide myself in you.
> Teach me to do your will,
> for you are my God;
> may your good Spirit
> lead me on level ground.

Will you follow the examples here and dedicate yourself to a daily quiet time? Avoid being a spiritual casualty. Seek the Lord daily and ask for guidance. Remember, *His* purpose is *our* purpose.

Homework Assignment 3:

1. Go to Section 2 of your Tool Kit, entitled "Tips and Tools for Quiet Time," to assist you in your daily quiet time. If you are not having a quality, consistent quiet time already, begin to incorporate some of the ideas offered here.
2. Try to establish this time daily by recording it in your weekly agenda.
3. Again, using Section 1 of your Tool Kit, fill in the events of "Week Two" *as they occur.* This will be a record of how you actually spent your time.
4. Keep this record with you this week, and be sure to use up the whole twenty-four hours for each day. Do not look back at your "Ideal Week" for reference.
5. Do this exercise to the best of your ability for seven consecutive days.
6. Once complete, you should be ready to begin Lesson 3.

Lesson 3:
The "E" Word

This chapter is a warning to all Super Moms out there. There is a virus among us called *Super Mom Syndrome*. Super Mom Syndrome presents itself in a beautiful package. It empowers Mom to, in a single evening, bake the entire alphabet in cookies several times over and hand-paint twenty-four plates for pre-kindergarteners so that tomorrow's snack time is educational and downright spectacular.

The infected mom shows up at school the next morning on time to deliver the snacks to the classroom. She and her child look like the cover of a *Children's Wear Digest* as they step out of their SUV. As they pass the office on the way to the classroom, Mom is stopped by the school secretary and recruited to be next week's morning child-checker for tardy and absent students. After agreeing to the job, Mom moves on to the classroom, where the delivery is made with pride. Her moment of recognition has arrived. It's only a matter of time before Miss Shapiro raves about the special treat in the weekly class newsletter. In fact, the newsletters should go home in backpacks today.

While visiting with the teacher, Mom learns that Miss Shapiro's class is gaining on the leader in the school fundraising competition. In a hurry to get to her next appointment, Mom writes a big check for twenty-eight rolls of unneeded gift wrap and moves the class into first place. This should also buy some major bonus points from the teacher that Mom can tuck away for future use.

As Mom leaves the school on the way to her Junior League service appointment, she manages to make arrangements to pick up another child for a play date later that afternoon and schedule an evening to take a meal to a neighbor who has recently had a baby. Wow! What a Super Mom.

But remember: this mom has the syndrome. Everything looks great on the surface, but the foundation is stricken with illness. The elaborate effort required for that very special snack came at a high cost—lack of sleep, low back pain, extra housework, and undone paperwork. The magazine cover look brought a big compromise in the morning routine that was accompanied by lots of yelling, scrambling, and what we like to call in the south, a hot mess left on the breakfast counter.

Moreover, there was not enough time to spend with God to pray over the order of the day. The extra volunteering at the school and the Junior League, and doing favors for friends and neighbors is time spent but not necessarily available. And that's not the only thing spent and not necessarily available. How about the funds to cover the fat check for all that gift wrap?

Looking from the revitalized perspective of my time belonging to God and His purpose, I began to ponder what it is that drives one to so fiercely pursue being Super Mom in the first place? Sure, we love our kids and want to do everything we can to equip them spiritually, physically, emotionally, and mentally. Scripture even tells us to do everything wholeheartedly, as if unto the Lord (Ephesians 6:7). But, seriously! Why do we do it this way? Why did *I* do it?

It's because Super Mom Syndrome is pandemic and it is caused by the "E" word—"Expectations."

There are many types of expectation. I think the most common one is the "WOPTOM" variety, otherwise known as "What Other People Think of Me." There are also the garden-variety strains:

- Keeping Up with the Joneses
- Overachiever Complex
- Giving My Kids What I Never Had
- Hostess with the Mostest
- I'll Never Admit It, but I'm Competing in the Social Climber Olympiad
- MENSA Needs Us
- Cutest Kid Competition
- We're Getting a Full Scholarship No Matter What These Private Lessons Cost
- Our Family Sits in the First Pew

And the ever-classic "One Up-ism."

It's ridiculous, but this is really what we do. Somehow we become entrapped in the process and worldly standards become the priority standards. We fail to recognize the roadblock we've created on the path the Lord has set before us. We fiercely build the world rather than the kingdom.

The good news is that there is a cure. We have to lay out everything we do before we take care of ourselves and serve God, and ask, "What is my motivation for these works?" When we are honest about our motivation, God is able to affirm in our hearts what is right and convict us of what is wrong. And so begins the process of our will coming into alignment with that of the Holy Spirit.

God entrusted these children to us. If we yield to His will the time he has given us to be in charge of them, he will faithfully enable us to get it right. Who cares what the neighbor thinks? Observing your faithfulness might just be the medicine she needs to cure her of Super Mom Syndrome too.

There are three key elements in Scripture to observe and put into practice to protect ourselves and to help us prioritize right expectations. First of all, remember whose time it really is. You were made for a purpose. You are not just "filler" in this universe. Second, God is the Author of time. If He says it is so, it is so. He knows you can do it and has already made a way. And third, it is your job to determine His will for you and live purposefully.

Write out the verses in the blanks below and answer the questions that follow each.

Ephesians 2:10

_____

_____

- Have you carefully considered the role God had in mind for you to play when He created the universe?

- What are your secret dreams, hopes, and desires?

- Do you have a special talent or gift?

Psalm 37:23-24

_____

_____

- Are you receiving affirmation that your efforts in a specific task or role are pleasing to the Lord?

- Is what you are doing bringing true joy or causing resentment? Explain.

- What do you need to trust the Lord for on your behalf?

Ephesians 5:15-17

_____

_____

- Have you checked your motives for your actions, and the motives of those around you?

- What doors of opportunity are being opened for you to act on God's behalf?

- What doors are being closed?

- Are you acting upon that little nudge He keeps giving you?

- Have you allowed your days to go to waste?

- Are you doing so many great things that you don't know which end is up?

It is entirely possible to be a Super Mom without having Super Mom Syndrome. Look and listen for opportunities to serve. Serve your family, your school, your church, and your community, not out of obligation or expectation, but out of love. Even though whatever you are involved in might be a really good thing, if it wasn't intended for you, let it go. If it is a right priority, God will empower you to complete the task. He has the power to turn Super Mom into Super*natural* Mom.

Lesson 4:
Momma Drama

Once we get over the unrealistic expectations we set as parents, we get real. We have to figure out how to get Play-Doh out of the carpet, remove an entire roll of tissue paper from the toilet bowl, and shoot miles of video footage of our little starlets without obstructing the view for all the other parents.

To that end, please note that this chapter embraces perfect practicality. It is not, however, Mary Poppins' guide to hosting the practically perfect tea party. It is intended to narrow your focus in order to prioritize the most important things, eliminate non-essentials, and save time by completing necessary items on the to-do list. Therefore, there are three basic principles to live by in order to survive the "Momma Drama."

Principle One: Take care of the big stuff first.

Principle Two: Learn to say no without suffering regrets.

Principle Three: Identify the task that you cannot say no to and break it down into a manageable system.

Principle One: Take care of the big stuff first

With all of the stuff we are trying to juggle, it is inevitable that we are going to drop something. Frankly, I would much rather drop a ball than a boulder . . . especially if it's going to end up on my foot.

To illustrate this point, I want to tell you a story about Sarah and Lilly. Sarah is a busy mom with a two-year-old son and a five-year-old daughter, Lilly, who is a kindergartener. Lilly has a favorite book series about "Girl Wonder." Sarah has been reading these stories to Lilly since Lilly was three years old. It has been a wonderful learning experience for Lilly, and a special bonding time for mother and daughter.

Every afternoon, Sarah waits in a carpool line, watching for Lilly to come out of the school and meet at their designated pick-up spot.

Lilly routinely walks out from under the kindergarten awning, down the steps and toward the angled walkway to the car.

However, one particular Monday afternoon was no ordinary afternoon. On that day, Lilly sprang from beneath the awning, took two steps down, and leaped from the stairs to the walkway. With eager anticipation, she hastened to the car. The latest book from the Girl Wonder series had arrived at the school library. The book was in high demand and Lilly got to be the first to check it out. She had four days to read the book before she had to return it because of its popularity. What a lucky girl to be the first to get her hands on the only copy from her favorite series! She squealed with delight as she asked her mom if they could read the book when they got home. Of course, Sarah agreed.

Before going home, Sarah decided to run a few errands. It would be convenient to let the baby nap in the car, and she could drop off some packages, pick up a few things for dinner, and grab the dry cleaning. Once they finally arrived at home and unloaded the car, the baby was screaming. He needed to be fed . . . and fed quickly! Sarah realized that the afternoon was nearly gone and supper needed to be started or everyone else in the house would soon be complaining of hunger as well.

Dinnertime came and went, and Lilly patiently and sweetly asked if they could now read the book. Sarah felt terrible that it had taken this long to get to the book. Attempting to manage her time well, Sarah instructed Lilly to go brush her teeth and get into her pajamas while Sarah put the baby to bed and cleaned up the dishes. Then she would meet Lilly in their favorite chair in the den underneath the reading lamp.

Sarah managed to complete her tasks and squeeze in a couple of phone calls. It was only a few minutes after Lilly's usual bedtime, but it was definitely worth an extra fifteen minutes to get in a little bit of the story. She kicked off her shoes and headed for the den to meet Lilly in the chair.

As Sarah walked into the room, she gazed upon Lilly in her Girl Wonder pajamas. Her little pink slippers had dropped on the floor beneath her feet. Lilly's golden curls lay across her face as her head slumped over on the chair. She was sleeping soundly with the book still pulled tightly into her chest.

It saddened and confused Sarah, for this was no ordinary Monday evening indeed. It was Thursday, and the book had to be returned the next morning. Where had the time gone? A few simple tasks had managed to steal away the opportunity to nurture the parent-child relationship and show Lilly that she was truly loved and that she and her mom had something special they shared.

As parents, our first priority is to love our children by providing for their basic needs. Whether we are able to do that in a lavish way or a simple way, we affect the hearts of our children. While we ourselves

> It's too big a sacrifice to achieve perfection in the details at the expense of tending to relationships.

cannot give them eternal salvation, we can equip them with truth and shape the content of their character on a daily basis. It's too big a sacrifice to achieve perfection in the details at the expense of tending to relationships. Furthermore, we must continue to strengthen our own relationship with God and put our core values ahead of our to-do list.

Christ, one's marriage, one's family, one's health . . . that is the big stuff. That is the stuff that has to come first. Lilly's mom, Sarah, only needed to put the big stuff first and everything else would have found its place.

Principle Two: Learn to say no without suffering regrets.

There are going to be many occasions when your resolve is tested in this area. As moms, we are often put on the spot. For example, if you are asked to host a last-minute event in your home but your kitchen floor hasn't seen a mop in weeks, you have a decision to make. You can say no and be done with it. Or, you can say yes and not worry about the kitchen floor. Either way, accept the decision for whatever it is with no regrets.

Regrets in this instance would be carrying around guilt for not agreeing to host the party, or forfeiting the right priorities in order to scrub the kitchen floor. Do you really want to establish your value based on how well the guests can see their reflections in the shine of your floor? I didn't think so.

It becomes a bit more complicated when faced with choices like giving up church attendance to play a sport, or allowing your child to attend a sleepover where there is little or no parental control. The answers seem obvious, but when you are in the moment and the whining, the puppy-dog eyes, and the "everyone else is doing it" commences, you are dealing with a whole different monster. Even other moms will try to convince you that it's okay just this one time. You might second-guess yourself, thinking perhaps you are being overbearing or unjust. Stay strong, think logically, and make a decision without going back on it.

The intention here is not to promote a position of inflexibility, but one of stability and rationality. This time it might be okay to run out for ice cream rather than going straight home. By all means go! But when it's not okay to go, it's not okay. You may have to be the "mean mom," but perhaps in the process you have instilled the importance of keeping a commitment or serving others in your child.

When it comes to our children, if we immediately gratify their requests on a regular basis, how are they to learn patience, perseverance through trials, or the dynamics of work and reward? More importantly, how are they going to learn to wait upon the Lord, seek His guidance, and trust Him when the answer is no?

Saying no also gives you the freedom to discover what it is you are really supposed to be doing for God. What if the thing you are supposed to be doing is resting—finding that still, small voice that guides you to your purpose and renews your strength to do the things you should with complete zeal?

> When it comes to our children, **if we immediately gratify their requests** on a regular basis, how are they to learn patience, perseverance through trials, or the dynamics of work and reward? More importantly, **how are they going to learn to wait upon the Lord, seek His guidance and trust Him when the answer is no?**

Truly letting go without suffering the regrets of saying no gives you freedom from the bondage of guilt. Guilt is an emotion introduced to the world by Satan in the Garden of Eden. Matthew 5:37 says, "Simply let your 'Yes' be 'Yes,' and your 'No,' 'No'; anything beyond this comes from the evil one." It is one of the most liberating truths to save any Super Mom out there.

Principle Three: Identify the task that you cannot say no to and break it down into a manageable system.

There are some things that can't be told no. Every mom has her own nemesis, but it can be tamed or even defeated. Step one in winning is to go ahead and face the battle head on. My particular nemesis is an endless pile of laundry. I have fully accepted the harsh reality that the chore of doing laundry is literally endless. It is an infinite circle of juice dribbles, mismatched socks, and grass-stained knees. At the very moment I am applying Spray 'N Wash to the clothes, my child is scooting her rear end across a dirt mound in the backyard. Having clearly identified laundry as the thing to which I cannot say no, I must implement a plan of action.

After much commiserating with fellow mommies, the consensus is that organization is key to staying ahead of the laundry game. A sorting system is essential. Soiled whites, colors, and towels (or whatever separation works for you) are each collected into individual hampers or baskets. As soon as one fills, it goes into the wash. If at all possible, fold that load as soon as the dryer cycle stops. That way, you can keep rotating clothes through the system as laundry accumulates.

Once the clothes are folded, make each child responsible for putting away her or his own laundry. It is okay to use the laundry to teach the children responsibility. There may be a bit of crumpling in the beginning, but teaching them the proper way to put the clothes away will ultimately lighten your load and save you tons of time. They can do it if you give them a chance. Even my three-year old knows in which basket to place her socks, pajamas, and T-shirts. How wonderful would it have been if your husband had automatically folded and put away his own laundry when you got married? If he did, you can thank his mother for that!

Here's the monkey wrench in your heavy-duty Whirlpool washer and dryer—*sports*. I cannot tell you how many times I had to dig dirty soccer socks out of the hamper or speed-dry a baseball jersey with the hair dryer before I figured this out. Keep the sports stuff out of the general laundry population during the season. Don't wait for the hamper to fill on these items, and know when your next game is scheduled. Another little Super Mom secret is that the practice wear can be worn stained and dirty. Save your time, energy, and OxiClean for the game clothes.

Last, but a most invaluable step in the game plan, is to designate a spot for equipment and accessories. Hats, cleats, gloves, and helmets need to have a special place to go for storage while not in use. It should be the same place every time. There are no exceptions. Otherwise, you'll be fifteen minutes late and your kid's pants are going to fall down rounding third base because he couldn't find the little elastic belt that goes with his uniform. And for Pete's sake, the extra socks, sliders, tights, and sports bra are worth the expense.

At this point, you may be wondering why you just read an entire section on managing the laundry. While far from glamorous, these routine chores are the day-to-day reality of motherhood. Thinking practically as opposed to striving for perfection affords you the opportunity to meet your family's needs and maintain your sanity.

As you live by these three principles, you free up time and energy to focus on the bigger picture, which includes discovering your calling, developing a clear vision, and living intentionally. As you develop these spiritual areas in your life, you become much more than a great mom. You become conditioned and available to pursue God's plan for your life.

Look for it. I bet it's bigger than your pile of laundry.

Homework Assignment 4:

1. Using the "Week Three" agenda from Section 1 of your Tool Kit, record the events of your week *as they occur.* The goal is to improve on "Week Two" and move closer to your "Ideal Week."

2. As you did last week, carry the weekly agenda with you for seven days, filling in all the blanks for the whole twenty-four hours of each day. Do your best to complete seven consecutive days and move on to Lesson 5.

3. Continue to incorporate a personal daily quiet time.

4. Compare and contrast the "Ideal Week" agenda with the "Week One" and "Week Two" agendas that you completed in Section 1 of your Tool Kit.

5. Answer the following questions:

   • How did you do?

   • What are some of the things you felt hit the mark, brought joy, or glorified the Father?

   • What big things do you need to put first?

   • What were your biggest time-wasters?

   • Did something in your day consistently cause frustration or interfere with your primary objective?

   • Is this something you can't say "no" to?

- What percentage of your time was spent seeking and acting on the will of the Father?

- What will you do to make changes next week?

The process of coming into obedience with our time takes work. Some may have had great success in keeping a perfect schedule, staying in alignment with God's will, and maximizing their gifts and talents. Most probably did not. It is a refinement process. The important thing is to make the effort every day and trust that you are not where you were, even if you are probably not where you want to be.

6. Make any adjustments in your "Ideal Week" agenda as you see appropriate.
7. If necessary, make a new ideal agenda using the extra "Ideal Week" provided in Section 1 of your Tool Kit.

Lesson 5:
Discovering Your Calling

Sometimes a task seems insurmountable—for instance, writing this study. There are much smarter people who should be doing this, people with better connections and abundant resources. And, certainly, there are more holy people who could be used by God.

I have heard that God does not call the equipped. He equips the called. Since I am writing this section of the study after having already completed most of it, I can say with confidence that this statement is true.

God will pursue you. He will lay something upon your heart and you will experience His nudging. Don't ignore His soft whisper nor hide from His loud calling. God chooses us because we are unique and set apart to accomplish His purpose. Be a willing participant in the life He has planned for you.

James 4:17 tells us that anyone who knows the good he ought to be doing and doesn't do it, sins. Making yourself available to receive His call is the prerequisite to realizing your vision. Listen to it, let God shape your plans, and follow through!

What seems impossible to man is possible with God. Looking at a situation through the Lord's eyes gives us the confidence to move forward and accomplish mighty acts in His name. He intervenes for those who honor Him in their work and seek to bring Him glory. God will accomplish His purpose through those who listen and respond to Him. Nehemiah was just such a man.

Read Nehemiah 1:1-4

In this passage, Nehemiah tells us when and where he is located. Translated, we know that he was an exile in Iran working in a position of honor for the king, whom at that time was Artaxerxes, King of Persia. A group of men came to Nehemiah from Judah and gave him news of Jerusalem and the Jewish remnant. His brothers who survived the exile and were back in Jerusalem were in "great trouble and disgrace" because the wall that protected them was broken down and the gates had been burned.

This news was very disturbing to Nehemiah, causing him to literally break down and cry. Nehemiah's weeping and mourning is evidence that God had greatly stirred his emotions on behalf of His people.

- What has the Holy Spirit brought into your presence that has attracted your attention or stirred your emotions?

- Is it possible that you have overlooked or dismissed an opportunity to do God's work?

Read Nehemiah 1:5-11

At this point, we know that Nehemiah had been mourning, fasting and praying for several days. Nehemiah's prayer in verses 5 - 11 is one of adoration, confession, claiming of promises, and sincere intercession for the Jewish people. Suddenly, in verse 11, Nehemiah boldly asks God to give him success by granting him favor in the presence of the king.

Nehemiah did not ignore what God had laid upon his heart. Instead, he took hold of it and turned to God in fervent prayer. And God answered.

Obviously, a large task was put on Nehemiah's heart. Where would he begin? He would begin right where he was. In verse 11, we see Nehemiah ask for success "today" and go on to simply state, "I was cupbearer to the king." He was ready to act right away in his present circumstance.

Some might delay obedience by assuming there is someone better, smarter, and stronger for the task. For others, obedience might be too costly. Nehemiah was in a respected, well-compensated position. Yet he was willing to walk away in obedience to God.

- Have you diligently sought God's direction and guidance in your prayer life?

- Are you willing to respond in obedience?

- From the place you are in right now, what action can you take?

Read Nehemiah 2:1-5

Here Nehemiah appears before the king with a heavy heart to deliver his wine. The king has not seen such a disposition in Nehemiah ever before. So the king asks Nehemiah about the sad expression on his face, saying that this is not illness but sadness of the heart.

Nehemiah shares his burden with the king concerning his homeland and the wall lying in ruins. The king asks Nehemiah what it is he wants. Nehemiah then makes his request.

Write out Nehemiah 2:5

_____

_____

Up to this point we have observed Nehemiah pouring out his heart and seeking the Lord for guidance. In verse 1:11, Nehemiah accepted God's task by asking for success in the presence of the king. His response here in 2:5 finally reveals to us how God replied to Nehemiah during his prayer and fasting. Now we know that the task is much larger than rebuilding the wall. It is rebuilding the entire city and restoring its heritage.

Though he was living and working *in* the world, Nehemiah was set apart because his heart and mind were not *of* the world. His heart and mind were open to the Lord's calling. Through Nehemiah's obedience and diligent seeking, God gave him more than a task in the midst of his everyday routine. God gave him a vision.

Homework Assignment 5:

1. Using the "Week Four" agenda from Section 1 of your Tool Kit, record the events of your week *as they occur.* The goal is to improve on "Week Three" and move closer to your "Ideal Week."
2. As you did in previous weeks, carry the weekly agenda with you for seven days, filling in all the blanks for the whole twenty-four hours of each day.
3. Continue to incorporate a personal daily quiet time.
4. Ask God to reveal His vision for you.

Lesson 6:
A Vision, A Mission

"I consider my life worth nothing to me, if only I may finish the race and complete the task the Lord Jesus has given me—the task of testifying to the gospel of God's grace." These are the words of the apostle Paul in Acts 20:24 NIV. It was a simple, powerful, and life-giving mission that started with a blinding vision from the Lord our God on an ancient road into Damascus. Other than Jesus himself, Paul is arguably the most influential person to have ever brought the good news of salvation to the Gentiles. Paul's vision became his mission. His mission was of God's choosing, and its far-reaching effects touch us today.

Like Paul, we are called to be set apart. Every Christian has a calling on his or her life. In my opinion, most people do not place the same value or significance on their life that God does. We tend to think that the important things are left to the popular and the powerful. Before you discount yourself or overlook any vision, great or small, let me point out the disciple, Ananias.

Ananias was a disciple in Damascus. Ananias had heard of Saul (who became Paul) and knew of Saul's reputation for ruthlessly persecuting Christians. Ananias was also aware that Saul had arrived in Damascus with legal authority over him and had the power to arrest him on the spot. Basically, Saul was the hammer and Ananias was the nail. But Ananias had his own call from the Lord. God commanded Ananias to go to Saul and place his hands upon Saul to restore Saul's sight.

Have you ever had a parent instruct you to come over to him while he was holding a switch from the nearest tree in his hand? You know what's going to happen if you walk over. Panic sets in to the pit of your stomach and you immediately begin a nervous negotiation to spare yourself from the situation. This was exactly Ananias' response. But the Lord said, "Go!"

Scripture tells us (Acts 9:17-18 NIV) that Ananias went to Saul and placed his hands upon him saying, "'Brother Saul, the Lord—Jesus, who appeared to you on the road as you were coming here—has sent me so that you may see again and be filled with the Holy Spirit.'" The scales fall from Saul's eyes, and "He got up and was baptized." After that, Saul became Paul, the greatest converted missionary for Jesus ever known.

The lesson here is that Ananias was also used by God. By the world's standards, Saul was the one in a powerful position. Saul could have destroyed Ananias, yet Ananias walked right up to him, put his hands on him, and changed the course of Saul's life, as well as millions of other lives, forever. Ananias was instrumental in fulfilling God's plan to use Paul to bring His message to the Gentiles.

Whether you are a Paul, an Ananias, a Nehemiah, or somebody's mom, taking control of the time you have been given every day in order to do that to which you have been called is hard work. In fact, your vision might seem downright overwhelming. It might even seem *under*whelming. The important thing is to make the effort every day. Living intentionally by being obedient in the small stuff ultimately and collectively builds the vision.

Keep in mind that not only does God give you the vision, He is also the Author and Perfecter of the faith (Hebrews 12:2) that enables you to live the vision. He turned a murderous Saul into saintly Paul. The enormity of Paul's mission was without end, carrying on still today.

In 2 Timothy 4:6-7 NIV, Paul writes, "The time has come for my departure. I have fought the good fight, I have finished the race, I have kept the faith." I cannot imagine the joy of finishing this well. Paul didn't have to be all things to all people. He didn't have to do it all by himself, and he didn't have to do it all right then. Paul was obedient to the call by God on his own life in his own given time. Through obedience, he gave life to the vision God gave him and pursued the resulting mission with absolute resolve. And it was epic.

As you work through this study, truths are revealed about who you are and where God has placed you. Your perspective of your role as a mom and a child of God will evolve, and the road map to your vision will become your mission.

At this point, you should have a good collection of weekly schedules to review that portray a snapshot of your life at the present. Reflecting on and analyzing what you have recorded has most likely shed some light on areas of strength and areas that need improvement. Now is the time to bring into focus your God-given purpose. Otherwise, there is a great risk that you will be very busy, yet wander aimlessly.

Seek His will fervently and ask Him to begin to make clear His vision for you. This vision will be unique to you and should be a reflection of that to which you feel God is calling you. To order your life in the will of the Lord is the only way you can truly be a Super Mom.

It is helpful to have a visual in mind of what the big picture looks like to you. Begin the process by identifying a *Simple Vision Statement.* A Simple Vision Statement is a basic, clear statement that sums up the whole of your time on earth. It's straightforward content broken down equals the sum of its parts minute-by-minute, hour-by-hour and day-by-day. It is your completed task.

Examples:

A) To have an impact on all those in my circle of influence for Christ through writing about His truth, and to have established a solid Christian legacy within my own family that will carry on for generations.

B) To minister to the needs of others through providing medical care and sharing the gospel with those whom I serve. To instill strong Christian values in my children so that they are equipped to go into the world under the full armor of God and successfully rise to the calling in their lives.

C) To use my resources to keep God present in the United States government and equip myself and others to spread the gospel to other areas of the world.

D) To model and mentor others in godly marriages. To personally assist in the restoration of broken families and be an effective proponent in initiatives to support this cause.

Proverbs 29:18 KJV says that where there is no vision, the people will perish. So what's your vision?

Homework Assignment 6:

1. Use Section 3 of your Tool Kit to formulate a Simple Vision Statement for yourself.
2. Using the "Week Five" agenda from Section 1 of your Tool Kit, record the events of your week *as they occur*. The goal is to improve on "Week Four" and move closer to your "Ideal Week."
3. As you did in previous weeks, carry the weekly agenda with you for seven days, filling in all the blanks for the whole twenty-four hours of each day.
4. Continue to incorporate a personal daily quiet time.

Lesson 7:
Intentional Living

God has given each of us roles in life. Some roles are relational by birth: father, mother, sister, cousin, etc. Other roles are relational by our own choosing or circumstance: husband, educator, neighbor, volunteer, or caregiver. And still others are part of our DNA. They are the ones that make us unique, the ones that we are born with by God's design. They are our gifts. Perhaps you are a prophet, an intercessor, or an encourager? Whatever the case, all of the roles we play can be developed and put into action to fulfill God's plan for our lives and bring Him glory in the process.

As you begin to think about the roles you play in life, carefully consider which ones are most important and which ones have the biggest impact on your daily living. Are they the same? Something as simple as not sharing a meal with your husband because of involvement at church, school, or a social organization can cause an imbalance in your priorities. None of these things are bad things, but are they appropriately prioritized in your Day-Timer? Allowing these little things to overshadow your priority roles and relationships is a compromise in values.

This practice of compromise quickly becomes a habit that spills over into all areas of our lives. Before we know it, our health, our children, our marriages, and even God are sitting on the back burner. We are no longer playing the leading role God intended for us. We lose our way when we let our *busy*ness become our *busi*ness.

To keep our balance, it is important to identify and focus on our priority roles and gifts. God gave them to us because He is a God with plans: plans to prosper and not to harm. Plans to give hope and a future! (Jeremiah 29:11 NIV) The sum of your roles, when played out with right priority, carry you to your purpose—*His* purpose.

I know that you have heard your mother, a grandparent, a teacher, or someone at some point in your life quote that famous, but absolutely true statement about you, "They broke the mold when they made you!" Take a moment to reflect on your life. Think about the following questions and write an answer for each.

- What are your five most important roles?

- If you could only perform three of the five, what three would they be?

- Now think about a typical day in your week. What three things do you spend the most time doing? Be specific. (Laundry, meal planning, computer use, working, playing with children, talking on phone.)

- Of the three things you spend the most time doing, which two could you cut out or significantly reduce?

Review your answers to these questions and seriously consider how you spend your time. Look at the roles you play as if you were an outside observer watching a movie of your life. Do the active roles you play in life define who you are, or does who you are define the active roles you play in life? To live intentionally, we must identify who God designed us to be and then apply it the roles we play and the time we've been given.

> Do the active roles you play in life define who you are, or does who you are define the active roles you play?

The question then is how to make that life application. We do it by setting clearly defined goals and practical objectives for reaching them. Once a goal is defined, it is not enough to just have it in your mind. Leaving it there makes for good daydream material and not much else. You have got to *write it down*. Research shows that people who have clearly defined goals and write them down are much more likely to accomplish them.

Furthermore, the steps to reach your goal must be established. These steps are the objectives you complete along the way. It is akin to drawing up a treasure map and following it step by step until you hit the "X."

The good Lord himself gives instruction in Habakkuk 2:2 ESV: "Write down the vision; make it plain on tablets so he may run who reads it." Proverbs 17:24 GNTA states that "an intelligent person aims at wise action but a fool starts off in many directions." If that's not convincing enough, the famous Yankee baseball player and coach, Yogi Berra, put it this way: "If you don't know where you are going, you'll end up someplace else."

As moms, we tend to have lofty goals like "raise godly children," but no real plan to bring them to life. We have to first measure our goals against Scripture and pray deliberately for God's guidance to lead us to the opportunities that He has pre-ordained. Next, we have to script out a practical plan for achievement. What are the steps required to get from point A to point B? Otherwise, we risk acting outside the structure of God's purpose for us. Outside of that structure is where we find ourselves very busy but bearing little fruit.

Think back to your vision statement. Based on that information, in combination with your personal life roles, what goals could be set to help you start intentionally living out your vision?

Remember Nehemiah. He was willing to give up his comfortable role with the king in order to take up his role as a member of an oppressed people. His vision of rebuilding a city wall restored the heritage of his people. It started with a stirring inspiration and was accomplished one task, one goal at a time. That's intentional living.

Homework Assignment 7:

1. Use Section 4 of your Tool Kit to identify all the roles you play. Be sure to include roles you were born into, roles you have chosen, and God-given roles such as spiritual gifts and extraordinary talents and interests. Follow the instructions in the Tool Kit to complete the entire form.

2. Use Section 5 of your Tool Kit to fill in the Goals Flow Chart. Be sure to include areas that do not currently exist but are needed to live a more balanced life and achieve your God-given purpose. Follow the instructions in the Tool Kit to complete the entire form.

3. Using the "Week Six" agenda from Section 1 of your Tool Kit, record the events of your week *as they occur.* The goal is to improve on "Week Five" and move closer to your "Ideal Week."

4. As you did in previous weeks, carry the weekly agenda with you for seven days, filling in all the blanks for the whole twenty-four hours of each day.

5. Continue to incorporate a daily quiet time.

6. Pray for God to reveal your priority roles, responsibilities, and perhaps any undiscovered gifts.

7. Ask God to help you define your goals and reveal the objective steps to achieve them.

Lesson 8:
Becoming Super Duper

"Dawg Day" is an expression borrowed from my aforementioned friend, Kimberly Knox. She is a committed Christian who was born and bred in the South. This good ol' Atlanta girl also happens to be a loyal Georgia Bulldog fan. I don't know whether or not her team loyalty led to this southern-fried acronym, but I like what it stands for and highly recommend implementing it into your life. It means *Day Alone with God.*

I find that the best way to truly have a Dawg Day is to completely remove myself from my usual environment. My most successful Dawg Day was on an interview trip with my husband. I left the children with a sitter and traveled to North Carolina with him. While he spent the day touring and talking with prospective employers, I skipped the sightseeing and stayed in the hotel room all day long. I turned my cell phone off, left my computer back in Georgia, blocked room calls, and hid the remote control in the back of a drawer. My only resources were my Bible, journal, pencil, and praise music.

Use your Dawg Day to reflect on and reassess your goals in light of God's plans for you. Praise Him openly and pray out all the contents of your heart. Make notes and meditate on His word. Allow your will to be realigned with the Holy Spirit. You will come through it with renewal, clarity, and inspiration to bring life to your vision.

You have accumulated a significant amount of data while doing the homework assignments in this short book. Now would be a great time for you to have a Dawg Day or even a mini-version of a Dawg Day. Just take a look at the layers of accomplishment that were established during the study:

1. A heart agreement that it is not your time but God's
2. Daily quiet time
3. Right and realistic expectations

4. Willingness to step up to your calling
5. A vision statement
6. Understanding of your roles
7. Well-defined goals and objectives, written down

Not only did you acquire all of these skills while working through the Tool Kit, but you put them into practice little by little each week as you used the Weekly Agenda Time Management Tool in Section 1. If you have truly opened yourself up to God's lead along the way, it is entirely possible that your feet are already firmly planted on the path of your God-given purpose.

Complete the final assignment in the Tool Kit knowing that God ordered and numbered your days before He even gave you life. Once you have finished each section and fully incorporated the Calendar Application, step back and realize that you have a plan of action. It's your own survivor's guide to saving Super Mom. You have been empowered by your Creator to be faster than a speeding bullet, more powerful than a locomotive, and able to leap tall buildings in a single bound.

Your time here on earth is a gift. Don't waste it! Intentionally live out the most important role assigned to you by God—being your kid's Super Mom!

Oh, how I long to hear, "Well done, thy good and faithful servant."

Kristi Walters

Homework Assignment 8:

1. Schedule time in your day planner for a mini DAWG day as soon as possible in order to complete the rest of this assignment.
2. Use Section 6 of your Tool Kit entitled "Calendar Application" to apply all the lessons learned in this study to your life.
3. Go live your calling.

Part 3:

Tool Kit

Section 1:
Weekly Agendas

Instructions for the **Ideal Week**:

Completely fill out the schedule the way it would look if everything in your life progressed perfectly all week. Use all the time available, even crossing out sections for sleep. Include all the big stuff (work, meetings, carpool, etc . . .) and the small stuff (send birthday cards, deliver gifts, pick up dry cleaning . . .). Put this page away and do not look at it again until instructed to do so.

About half way through this study you will mostly likely feel the need to completely re-negotiate your time in an ideal week. This is why you have been provided a second blank ideal week page. You will be prompted to create a new ideal week if needed at the appropriate time in the study. Use a pencil. It's a refinement process.

Instructions for **Weekly Agendas**:

Keep this schedule with you all week. Fill in the blanks as they occur to the best of your ability. DO NOT write down what you think is going to happen. Write down what actually happens. It is helpful to fill in the blanks at several points in the day so that nothing gets left out. For example, right after kids leave for school record all the events of the morning. During lunch fill in everything that has happened since your last log, and so on; mid-afternoon, evening, bedtime . . . Again, it is a good idea to use a pencil.

---

5   Follow Saving Super Mom on Facebook for free downloadable forms from the Tool Kit

Ideal Week

	Mon	Tue	Wed	Thur	Fri	Sat	Sun
5am							
6am							
7am							
8am							
9am							
10am							
11am							
12pm							
1pm							
2pm							
3pm							
4pm							
5pm							
6pm							
7pm							
8pm							
9pm							
10pm							
11pm							
12am							

Notes

Ideal Week

	Mon	Tue	Wed	Thur	Fri	Sat	Sun
5am							
6am							
7am							
8am							
9am							
10am							
11am							
12pm							
1pm							
2pm							
3pm							
4pm							
5pm							
6pm							
7pm							
8pm							
9pm							
10pm							
11pm							
12am							

Notes

Week One

	Mon	Tue	Wed	Thur	Fri	Sat	Sun
5am							
6am							
7am							
8am							
9am							
10am							
11am							
12pm							
1pm							
2pm							
3pm							
4pm							
5pm							
6pm							
7pm							
8pm							
9pm							
10pm							
11pm							
12am							

Notes

Week Two

	Mon	Tue	Wed	Thur	Fri	Sat	Sun
5am							
6am							
7am							
8am							
9am							
10am							
11am							
12pm							
1pm							
2pm							
3pm							
4pm							
5pm							
6pm							
7pm							
8pm							
9pm							
10pm							
11pm							
12am							

Notes

Week Three

	Mon	Tue	Wed	Thur	Fri	Sat	Sun
5am							
6am							
7am							
8am							
9am							
10am							
11am							
12pm							
1pm							
2pm							
3pm							
4pm							
5pm							
6pm							
7pm							
8pm							
9pm							
10pm							
11pm							
12am							

Notes

Week Four

	Mon	Tue	Wed	Thur	Fri	Sat	Sun
5am							
6am							
7am							
8am							
9am							
10am							
11am							
12pm							
1pm							
2pm							
3pm							
4pm							
5pm							
6pm							
7pm							
8pm							
9pm							
10pm							
11pm							
12am							

Notes

Week Five

	Mon	Tue	Wed	Thur	Fri	Sat	Sun
5am							
6am							
7am							
8am							
9am							
10am							
11am							
12pm							
1pm							
2pm							
3pm							
4pm							
5pm							
6pm							
7pm							
8pm							
9pm							
10pm							
11pm							
12am							

Notes

Week Six

	Mon	Tue	Wed	Thur	Fri	Sat	Sun
5am							
6am							
7am							
8am							
9am							
10am							
11am							
12pm							
1pm							
2pm							
3pm							
4pm							
5pm							
6pm							
7pm							
8pm							
9pm							
10pm							
11pm							
12am							

Notes

Week _____

	Mon	Tue	Wed	Thur	Fri	Sat	Sun
5am							
6am							
7am							
8am							
9am							
10am							
11am							
12pm							
1pm							
2pm							
3pm							
4pm							
5pm							
6pm							
7pm							
8pm							
9pm							
10pm							
11pm							
12am							

Notes

Section 2:
Tips & Tools for Quiet Time

Your quiet time is your opportunity to have one-on-one communication with God. True communication involves both parties talking, listening and sharing ideas. There are two simple elements to have an effective quiet time: **Prayer** and **God's Word**. There is one very easy way to link these together . . . a **journal**.

Tips for a successful quiet time:

- Time
- Place
- Specifics
- Scripture

Time—Set a standing appointment for your quiet time. It is best to choose the same time every day. This will aid in establishing a habit. In the beginning you may only use a few minutes, but as you mature into your quiet time you may need to allow more time. This is your most important meeting of the day. You have an appointment with the King!

Place—Choose a solemn place free of interruption or distraction to have your quiet time. Do not turn on the television or attempt to have quiet time in your bed. I can practically guarantee that you will end up day dreaming or falling asleep. Stage your quiet time area to set you up for success. Keep a bag or basket with your Bible, journal, pen and perhaps a study guide in the place you have chosen.

Specifics—A common obstacle to effective prayer is indiscriminate thought or getting lost in a prayer loop that leads to daydreaming. This is where your journal becomes vital. Either make a list of the things you want to pray about and lift them one by one. Or, write out your prayers as if writing a letter to God.

Scripture—The Bible is the living, breathing, inspired word of God spoken directly to us. God uses it to reveal His character to us that we might know Him and be saved by His grace. It is without question that we must read or hear His word everyday for it is life-giving. The following is a list of suggested ways to incorporate daily scripture reading into your quiet time.

- Verse of the Day calendar
- Bible Study Guide
- One Year Bible
- Devotional Book
- Scripture Memory cards

Whatever method you choose, meditate on His word and ask yourself questions. Record any revelations you receive.

- What do the words mean?
- What is the biblical truth in this scripture?
- How does this apply to me?
- Are there steps to be taken?

Whether in prayer or in study, take time to listen carefully for God's response. These are usually quiet nudges from deep within your heart, but don't rule out a resounding command. Measure what you think God's response is against scripture, circumstance and wise, Godly counsel.

Be sure to review your journal regularly. Make note of when and how God answered prayers. Write down revelations received during scripture study and meditation. Watch your relationship with God grow and become well adept at recognizing His voice.

Section 3:
Simple Vision Statement

Look and listen with eager anticipation for a prompting from God. As you pray and seek God's will, ask yourself these questions:

1. What are my gifts and talents?
2. What is my motivation?
3. Is this consistent with scripture?
4. How does this compare with the desires of my heart?
5. Have I really talked to God about this and trusted Him to guide my steps?
7. What is keeping me from obedience in this area?
8. What verse inspires me daily as a Believer?

Considering all of the answers above, write a brief description of what you think God has called you to do for His purpose. Be sure to incorporate anything from elsewhere in this study that has impacted your thoughts about your purpose and your goals in life. Continue to refine this description until you feel you have defined your vision statement.

Vision Statement

Section 4:
Life Roles

Instructions:

1. Complete the Life Roles worksheet by filling in information down one column at a time. First, fill in the *second* column with all of your life roles. Include those by birth, choice, inheritance or giftedness.

Example:

	Role
____	*Sister*
____	*Candy Striper*
____	*Intercessor*

2. Write a very short description of how you think you might be called to fill each role. Do this in the *third* column.

Example:

____	*Sister*	*Support Sara in career; encourage Christian walk*
____	*Candy Striper*	*Be on time; minister to the sick and lost*
____	*Intercessor*	*Establish weekly prayer time for school*

3. Grade yourself reflecting your performance of each role in the *first* column.

Example:

B	*Sister*	*Support Sara in career, encourage Christian walk*
A	*Candy Striper*	*Be on time, minister to the sick and lost*
C	*Intercessor*	*Establish weekly prayer time for school*

Life Roles

——	————	————————————————
——	————	————————————————
——	————	————————————————
——	————	————————————————
——	————	————————————————
——	————	————————————————
——	————	————————————————
——	————	————————————————
——	————	————————————————
——	————	————————————————
——	————	————————————————
——	————	————————————————
——	————	————————————————
——	————	————————————————
——	————	————————————————
——	————	————————————————
——	————	————————————————
——	————	————————————————
——	————	————————————————

---

[6]   Follow Saving Super Mom on Facebook for free downloadable forms from the Tool Kit

Section 5:
Goals Flow Chart

Instructions:

1. In the Goals Flow Chart provided, use the first column to list separately each major area of life. Use the following applicable categories: **Spiritual, Mental, Physical, Social, Financial, Marriage, Family, and Career**. You may identify additional categories by reviewing your list of roles. The idea is to be as well balanced as possible using the categories that are best suited for you. Ask the Lord to bring to mind those things that He intends for you to include.
2. In the second column of the goals chart write in your goal for that category. Be sure to make reference to your Vision Statement when formulating goals. *A goal is the long-term desired result.*
3. In the third column of the goals chart write in the objective for your goal. *The objective is the short-term step or steps taken to achieve the goal.*

Example:

Spiritual	1. Mature relationship with God 2. Know and act on His will	a) Daily quiet time b) Memorize scripture c) Act on one Godly nudging each week
Physical	1. Lower cholesterol 2. Maintain healthy weight	a) Increase fiber intake b) Sign up and train for one 10K c) Join run club 3x per week

Goals Flow Chart

Section 6:
Calendar Application

Materials Needed:

- One-year calendar
- Personal day timer (the one you use daily to track appointments)
- Completed Goals Flow Chart
- Completed Life Roles worksheet
- Weekly Agenda Ideal Week worksheet
- Best week of your Weekly Agendas worksheets

Instructions:

1. Using your Goals Flow Chart and Life Roles worksheet, identify any goals to which a target date for completion can be assigned. Write each one on your one-year calendar.

    Example:

    <u>C</u>   <u>Intercessor</u>   <u>Establish a weekly prayer time for school</u>

    Implement by marking your calendar for every Monday at 7:50am to drop off the children and stop to pray over the school and students for 5-10 minutes. Make this a weekly recurring event.

2. Review the objectives on your Goals Flow Chart and the information on your Life Roles worksheet. Identify any items that are steps to reach a goal. Write each one on your one-year calendar.

Example:

Family	1. Be a Christian influence on my nephew	a) Communicate on regular basis b) Plant scripture in heart c) Be an encourager

Schedule a telephone call to your nephew on his birthday. Two weeks before final exams begin, make an appointment to shop for care package items. Two days later make time to package the items with a note of encouragement and mail the package. Plan a day to visit your nephew's home and share a bible verse or give a devotional book. Write these on your calendar and keep these appointments as if they are the only spot your hair dresser has open for a highlight.

3. Transfer all the data on your one-year calendar into your day timer.

4. Review your Ideal Week worksheet along with your selected Weekly Agenda worksheet. Plug in all the remaining activities in your day timer that give you the best chance for success. Include your daily quiet time as a standing appointment. Omit items that squeeze out the things to which you are called and so ordained to do.

5. Choose one or two days in the year to have a DAWG day.

"For I know the plans I have for you, declares the Lord, plans to prosper you and not to harm you, plans to give you hope and a future."

Jeremiah 29:11 NIV

Bibliography

1 Alice In Wonderland John Carroll.
2 John Randolph, U.S. Senator 1825-1827
3 Merriam Webster www.merriam-webster.com
4 Billy Graham, "Completing the Task God Gives Us" *Decision Magazine*, www.billygraham.org (October 1, 2008)